A Wind's Whisper

Alex Tilley

BookLeaf Publishing

Presentation by *BookLeaf Publishing*

Web: www.bookleafpub.com

E-mail: info@bookleafpub.com

ISBN: 978-93-95950-22-0

First edition 2022

DEDICATION

My pops, who carried me into the world of books and put the energy of creativity into my soul.

My mom, who carried me into this world and wouldn't feel any shame in reminding me of it.

Natalie, always.

PREFACE

Don't look for me.

Don't look for soul secrets here.

Just look for you.

And hey, if you don't find any of yourself in these words, then that piece of you is just waiting somewhere else.

Autumnal Hunger

Do you seek words that will change you?
Do you seek the soul of the sound?

Where the wind's whispers derange you,
Do you believe that you've been found?

In the shadows of shaking boughs,
Have you yet witnessed truths around?

If the stories never change you,
They too will diminish and brown.

Walls of Bone

Snakish eyes of brown,
Powdered cheeks and nose.
Black thong.
Pink shades.
I will build your home.

Raven hair of black,
Sharpened chin of stone.
White smile.
Purple pants.
You'll never be alone.

Maggot coloured polish,
Painted on your toes.
Sushi dates.
Crude jokes.
You've built up walls of bone.

Scorpion edged laughter,
Outlasting all your throes.
Virgo scales.
Chewed nails.
Will you put down your phone?

Look!

The leaves are changing colour.
Summer crowns.
Falling down.
He will leave you prone.

What is death if all things die?

I walked the cemetery, graves unmarked.
Stories told, and stories forgot.
I read my book and drank my tea.
Will there be anything left of me?

Bayonets once drawn with painted blades,
There's art in death upon the glades.
He buckled helmet among the tents,
Brothers, sisters, and warriors bent.

I imagined curled toes in their boots.
Blood and mud where once men stood.
Rusted rifles, dirty cheeks. I drank my tea.
Will there be nothing left of me?

He grabbed his reins and pet his horse,
Her nose was soft, but her mane was coarse.
A stud to die upon the plain,
Cavalry lost in a foreign domain.

Poppies blood upon the stones.
People jogging, babies in tow.
I checked my phone, sipped my tea.
What are the thoughts of they to me?

Swollen fingers, sooty eyes.
In war, what is death if all things die?
He mounts his steed, rifle high.
In war, what is death if all things die?

I check my watch, it's time to go.
The poppies follow, caught in the wind.
Tomorrow I'll return with another tea.
I'll forget you, but will you remember me?

Caramel Macchiato

It's colder than I remember,
But it's nice to be with you.
Caramel macchiato?
How about we make it two.
You run me through your stories,
I wonder if they're true.
I tell you all about me,
There are only a few who knew.

We talk until it's morning,
Wishing it was Spring.
We listened to the wind,
It knows everything.
Your favourite number's four,
I suppose that mine is eight.
Dinner plans?
That sounds grand.
Hurry or we'll be late.

I wish that you ran deeper,
But the flaw is one with me.
I let you play your song,
But you trusted me with three.
You told me of your loves,
I hate them to this day.

I showed to you my soul,
You never saw me the same.

It's warmer than it was,
I think because of you.
Caramel macchiato?
How about we make it two?

Free

The wind carried through the valley, like the bellow of a god.
Freckled shoulders, a pimple between your breasts,
Masked beneath your knitted sweater.
Where once was love, the wind has stolen.

Tree top flames, birds' homes burning, leaves falling like remnant ashes.
His soul of music was inflamed by your fears,
As he played the tune of your heart.
Have you thought of letting him spread his wings?

The trees were anchored by their roots, hold fast or accept your fate.
Sly smiles and a pretty dress won't save you.
You think this is satisfying?
He can't carry you through this torn valley.

Lifted shingles, hellish screams caught in a whirlwind of debris.
I can shield you, but you'll need to tie your hair.
Singing and dancing is your dream,
If I carry you, will you carry me?

The wind lashes like a whip. It's okay to cry,
please just stay.
He'll look back, and you will hear his name
again.
I'll have forgotten to know hate,
But the green eye'd monster will feast on me.

He who reaches through your soul, into a place
he doesn't know.
You feel the fingers playing your softened
strings.
Have you forgotten how to hate?
I see now that time has played me.

Kraken (Part I)

"Have ye felt the brittle bone-teeth of a winter sea's breeze?
Yer baby skin would crinkle like a walrus's if ye'd sail with me.
Eh, look at yer hands. Like polished marble.
Ye don't have the mind for netting lobster from here to St. Anthony.

"Ye once did sail a whaler, but let me tell ye there b'y,
Ye ain't here yet a sailor, until ye seen the cold limbed maiden cry.
There's a darkness in the water: Black Dread.
She'll look to pull ye under, she'll be the only who wilt see ye die."

The man with bull-shoulders spoke to me with a beer sloshing in his grip.
His eyes sparkled like a supernova.
His skin was a sandy grit.

He looked upon me with the gaze of a monarch, weighing my resolve.
He brought the foamed draft to his lips and drank;

I was more than he could solve.

“There’s not a thing ye could offer, to sail with us ahead.
Yer better off in a library, as the maiden would have ye dead.
An oceanic wyvern with snake limbs.
I’m not sure ye understand, the trouble ye’d begin,” the man had said.

“Ye’d set a course for disaster, a ship caught in a cleft.
Cold nights, salt burn, rashes upon your face, ye’d dwindle to nothing left.
She’d catch a scent and curse us man and crew.
She’s a maiden to the wave, bound to the wind, she’ll leave us all bereft.”

I stared upon the man, watched his coloured eyes. I wish I listened then.
I heard a pretty voice, one not well known.
It told me of where and when.

Her small hand was cold upon my own, her whisper was a breath of wind.
She spoke of things I didn’t understand.
Her face was oval and thin.

She never left her whisper, as if yelling from afar.
"A man who carries suffrage without courage, is that the man you are?"
I wish I had spoke my truth to her then.
She clasped my hand and softly whispered, "to live, the soul is to be scarred.

"Are you afraid, sailor? Listening to these salted men?"
"B'y, watch this slithering water snake's tongue, shedding rotten things again.
A wandering crow without a feather;
She'll peck upon your skull, and your decaying bones among the heathen."

This woman who understood my thoughts left no doubt for mistrust. She smiled.
Her eyes plummeted deeper than the deep.
I felt nothing of beguile.

Her voice was of the wind, and the wind pushed me to sea.

Cold Winter Breathing

Are you still afraid?
Tugging at your scalp.

Breathe.

Breathe.

Do you feel it now?

Breathe.

Breathe.

Smoke plumes of released fear.

Breathe.

I hear your chest filling.
Yes!

Breathe.

Maybe you just want to be seen?

Breathe.

Breathe.

Dark Matters

Philanthropic stabbing attack.
Have you seen the corpses around Robert Frost?
Who reads poetry anyway.

Salivating surgeon knooses.
Were you serviced by Dr. Kevorkian?
Who enjoys this show anyway.

Game of… bones.
Faye Valentine or Faye Reagan?
We're all alone anyway.

Celestial black matter.
It's so cold in here.
I've been breathing sickness anyway.

Resurrecting Klopfer corpses.
They'll be frostbitten from their graves.
Their ice bones are brittle anyway.

Derealized human sacrifices.
Have you forgotten God?
He's forgotten you anyway.

Alzheimers isn't a fucking joke,

So the good doctor gets my vote.
What was I saying anyway?

Overrepresented black boys.
You still think it's a joke?
Who am I to say anyway.

Forgotten child rapes.
Do not say that word.
Who is listening anyway.

Blasphemous inertia.
But I'm so tired…
I never slept much anyway.

Late-Winter Walks

Dog's breath, for panic attacks.
Cold drinks to help me relax.
Therapy in back room talks.

Sour humour I understand.
The world froze when I brushed your hand.
I hope you're watching the clock.

Jane Austen is the name of the day.
Fall on your knees to make me stay.
Wind caught snow on February walks.

Troubled ghosts in both our heads.
Skin is soft from tears we shed.
My mistakes are yours to mock.

Hard cut good-byes.
I can see it in your eyes.
Let's just go one more block.

Kraken (Part II)

I'm writing in this journal, and then shouting it to the darkened sea.
There's nothing to return to back at home,
I pray the crew takes to me.

The woman who understood me, her name, a man could never forget.
Eyes like a clouded winter nebula,
They held me like a planchette.

"Are you frightened?" she whispered, somehow louder than the waves.
"Fear is for children, and I took you for a man.
You think me depraved?
I am not any person you yet know,
I have seen beyond that what you see as dark and light. I am no slave.

"I am the master of myself. I am deeper than black,
Do not call me woman, for I am more than your ideation's lack-"
"Stop yer hollering water snake woman,
'Til ye can haul line handsomely, ye best away as we get tackin'."

Beauty's eyes scolded the Captain, her black
cloak breaking upon the wind.
The warmth of her fury tempered my heart,
As the sea frost burned my skin.

The ship, while tacking, rocked against the
barrage of waves breaking the stern.
Dark beauty gripped my arm like catfish teeth,
With a fear one could discern.

"Ahoy! There she is lads: Black Dread! Ho!
Shift the boom with me."
Suddenly, like a geyser bursting forth, a black
snake-limb fled the sea.
"Heave the line. B'y! Heave!" the Captain called
out.
Water exploded, turning sailors to jetsam,
raining as debris.

Panic had blinded me, as Beauty and I fell away.
Icy burns were forgotten, as black arms twisted
among the forestays.
I heard Beauty laugh, as she caught the prow.
"I am here, mother Kraken, with an offering of
freshly caught prey."

I didn't let her finish, as I pushed her overboard
to her end.

Winter sea's tentacles crashed around me,
It was more than I could fend.

Her voice screamed from the water, and I
followed it below.

As Snow Melts, Winter Cries

Nights still cold after dusk in the church.
There I saw melted snow off the birch.
There's a whore dancing close,
Pierced nipples. She's a rose.
How she walks, head aimed low, with a lurch.

Without home, without self. I smell death.
Shameless stare watching me take a breath.
Funeral hands turned cold.
Acts of youth, now she's old.
Curled and frayed splitting ends, skin like meth.

Barrel fires lighting glass among pews.
There I watched, swollen bone points at you.
Lawless lust in God's home,
Take my hand, take my bones.
I will come with clasped souls in a spew.

You want more, I gave less than your eyes.
Desperate taboo'd touch on my thigh.
Hungered thirst needing more.
Thick hip sway's sexy gore.
Escaping boney grip and your stye.

Whispering spring time wind, let it end.

I beg you, set me free to transcend.
Cracked stained glass shields my face,
As I watch fallen grace.
Do not trust in my words, I’m no friend.

As Dawn Rises

There is more than darkness in this world.
Plains of lavender, and colours that swirl.
There is hope amidst the suffering.
The rising of dawn on a returned Spring.

Beyond light there is home, there is you.
Breathing peonies bring forth life anew.
You are called to take lead, let me come.
I shall follow you, as my bones grow numb.

Marching child in the streets, calling hail.
I shall hoist the men, we will take to sail.
Languid fools will lift now to the fore,
Not just for beauty, but because it's yours.

Light or dark take us now to fresh skys.
Although you are short, hope is in your eyes.
Give me strength, let me come, I will fight.
As the dawn rises, and then sets for night.

Let me come. Let me come. Call to me.
Beyond dark, beyond new peonies.
Take my hand! Please, take it, for I'm trapped.
Will you not save me from this bondage wrap.

The sun rose, now it sets upon doom.
Is it destiny that has betrayed you?
Dwindle here in the black dying light.
'Though dawn rises, you're alone in the blight.

I call Ovid and to others outside my turgid shell.
That you'll lift me higher lest I'm doomed to
hell.

Nightstalker

Rain slapped the fogged windshield.
Your pills on hand tonight.
I try to sleep, I've gone too deep.
Flowers hungry for life.
Softly knocking knuckles,
At the car door window,
Dark eyes watch me, white teeth smile too.
Goosebumps up my elbow.

"Hi there, my name's Marcus. My car broke down, can you… help?"
I checked my watch, fifteen past twelve. The moon was still out.
I sighed deeply, knowing I could never say no.
I threw a quick simper, unclicked my belt and rose.

The rain abused my head.
Splashing on black pavement.
I turned to see him following,
I don't know where he went.
Rain sheets consumed darkness.
I tried to shield myself.
Yellow slit eyes opened up wide.
I knew he broke his stealth.

What once was a man, slithered like a serpent
prowling.
Dementor demon, bat-like shadow with claws
crawling.
Red lips pulled back, white teeth dripping
hunger and death.
It jumped forward. I crashed backward. I felt its
breath.

Rain slapped my forehead,
As it sank its teeth into my neck.
Sweet salivating lust pulsating.
I was warm and wet.

It licked the wound, and stood over me,
Black shape a wafting curtain.
I couldn't breathe… I couldn't scream…
Death was certain.

Diminishing Returns

Have you forgotten hope, silent scholar?
There's a place for ones like us.
Maybe you'll enjoy being collared.
Quiet down now, restrain your fuss.
If it's truth that you've been seeking,
You'll find that nothing's free.
Watch the words you've been speaking,
Actions don't fall far from the tree.
Hope speaks through your learning.
Live for hope. Die for hope.
Fight with spirit's yearning.
Sheets of silver glass staring back at me.
A monster or a mask, no wonder I don't sleep.

It Smells Like Rain

Last Spring’s rain,
Patters on the stone.
Let's just stay,
I know you’re alone.
Baby coos,
and unwashed lunch bowls.
There’s a fool,
Talking without soul.

Smiling friends,
Watching you dwindle.
Silent cries,
Over sopped kindle.
Ashy coals;
The fire is dead.
All knowledge,
Went straight to his head.

Sleep silent,
Listen to the rain.
You shall see,
A new Spring again.
Don’t touch me,
That’s not why I’m here.
Just listen,

There's more than just fear.

Hate consumes
Once inside your veins.
Please breathe free,
as you'll bloom again.

Sleep now, safely here.
Rest until you see.

Message in a Bottle

I started my Summer with Bukowski,
Unrealizing his depravity.
Toilet bowls, and hurt backs.
What a Summer this will be.

Cigarette burns hidden in the sand.
Summer songs by your favourite band.
I'm looking for something,
And I refuse to be just friends.

Explicit morose kisses with your tongue.
Sweat saturated towels to be rung.
You drink wine, I smoke weed,
We'll take the hit into our lungs.

Verbal diarrhoea running down your chin.
Pretentious poet's woes inside your trash bin.
I feel small, make me tall.
Hopefully this excrement gets lost in the wind.

Sunflower

You look at me and smile.
Ocean blue eyes, with elven hair.
I don’t fear life with you.

I see and know what is.
Duck pond visits, and ice cream trucks.
Sunflower fields with you.

How much do I reveal?
Do you know what? This is not love…
This is pure life with you.

Loving can be fickle:
There as a flame, gone in a flash.
Life is treasure with you.

Yellow No Frills shop carts.
Dorito bags, Pizza Nova,
I’ll eat the worst with you.

Take those big jumps sweet girl,
I will be here to catch your fall.
It is true life with you.

Natural Intimidation

What do you think an old woman sees when she looks at you?
Clouding cataracts won't hide your forked tongue.
Speak truth to me, for lies seep out of pores like pus.
People are intimidated thinking a lady has entered the room.
Men become enslaved and women fear a wise one so young.
You don't deceive me, even though you believe that you must.

Why do you let me talk like this?
Cracked stone foundations leaking.
Am I emptying or am I drowning?
I caught your gaze for a second too long…
Spider eyes.
Black lips.
You had more to say,
But I had to look away.
Now Summer is almost gone.

Strange State of Affairs

A creature of your world, yet he's afraid to
consume your flesh?
You're honest and you're happy, and yet expect
nothing less.
Explore yourself freely, for you have been
self-oppressed.
You will set you free.

This Is Home Now

Shedded snake-skin pants.
Methamphetamines.
Blood stained boots and hands.
I am more than these.

Tinted windowed car,
Cruising Venice Beach.
Friends in Kandahar.
Children run from me.

This is not a show.
Do you hear that sound?
That's the laundry mat.

You're the best of us.
Take us all by storm.
Don't be treasonous,
Don't bend to the swarm.

I am broken now,
Bones baked by the sun.
Crown upon your brow,
Desert flower gun.

This is not a poem.

Don’t you hear it now?
Puke stains on your shoes.

Wiser than before,
So when pain comes by,
Open up that door
To learn how you’ll die.

Purple clouded sky
Tainted memory,
If I say good-bye,
Will you let go of me?

Broken femur bone,
With your body found
At the grocery store.

Insatiable

Tales are oft too long,
But the words I ache to hear
Have yet to be found…

www.ingramcontent.com/pod-product-compliance
Lightning Source LLC
Chambersburg PA
CBHW051747130826
49812CB00033B/1034
9789395950220